That's Odd!

by Alice Boynton

Red Chair Press   Egremont, Massachu

Look! Books are produced and published by Red Chair Press:

Red Chair Press LLC   PO Box 333   South Egremont, MA 01258-0333

FREE Educator Guides at www.redchairpress.com/free-resources

Publisher's Cataloging-In-Publication Data

Names: Boynton, Alice Benjamin, author.

Title: That's odd! / by Alice Boynton.

Description: Egremont, Massachusetts : Red Chair Press, [2021] | Series: Look! books : What a job | Interest age level: 005-008. | Includes index and resources for additional reading. | Summary: "In this book, readers learn about the skills required for some unusual and really odd jobs such as professional taste and odor testers, dog walkers, and trapeze artists"--Provided by publisher.

Identifiers: ISBN 9781634408318 (library hardcover) | ISBN 9781634408356 (paperback) | ISBN 9781634408394 (ebook)

Subjects: LCSH: Occupations--Juvenile literature. | Dog walking--Vocational guidance--Juvenile literature. | Sensory evaluation--Vocational guidance--Juvenile literature. | Aerialists--Vocational guidance--Juvenile literature. | CYAC: Occupations. | Dog walking--Vocational guidance. | Sensory evaluation--Vocational guidance. | Aerialists--Vocational guidance.

Classification: LCC HF5381.2 .B69 2021 (print) | LCC HF5381.2 (ebook) | DDC 331.702 [E]--dc23

Photo credits: Shutterstock except for the following: pp. Cover, 1, 6, 7, 15, 17, 19; p. 10: Michael Dunlea/Alamy; p. 11: dpa picture alliance archive/Alamy; p. 16: Jim West/Alamy

Printed in United States of America

0920 1P CGS21

Table of Contents

Many jobs are important. But some jobs are not regular and may even be odd. Which of these odd jobs would you most like to do?

Dog Walker

Have you ever seen someone walking lots of dogs? That's a dog walker at work. A walker knows how to handle many dogs. Come! Stay together! The dogs are safe and happy. They get lots of **exercise**. So does the dog walker!

Good to Know

A dog walker must clean up after the dogs. It is part of the job.

A good dog walker must give attention to each dog.

Sky Writer

Pilots fly planes. Some pilots write **messages** in the sky, too. The plane gives off smoke. The smoke forms letters or shapes. If the letter is T, the pilot flies in a straight line. If it's O, the pilot flies in a circle. Imagine writing a heart in the sky. Wow!

Zoo Dentist

Zoo animals need **dental** care, just like we do. Some animals can be trained to open wide. It's easy to brush their teeth. But what if a tiger or wolf has a cracked tooth? Those sharp teeth can bite!

Say "Aahhh."

Zoo dentist to the rescue! The dentist gives the animal a special shot. The animal falls asleep. The dentist's hands are safe. The dentist can fix the problem. When the animal wakes up, no more toothache!

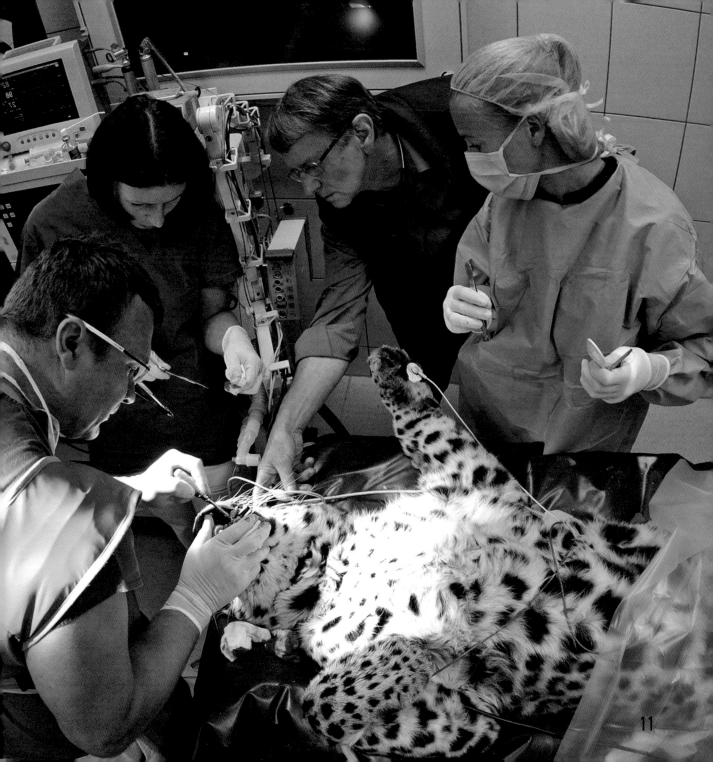

Sound Effects Artist

Movies are full of sounds. There's talking, of course. Sometimes you hear rain, too. And maybe thunder or fire. A sound effects artist makes the sounds. How? You may be surprised.

To make sounds, the artist uses **common** things. Try these sounds!

Rain: Sprinkle uncooked rice on a cookie sheet.

Fire: Crunch paper in your hands.

Thunder: Jiggle a sheet of metal like a cookie sheet.

15

Snacks Inspector

Snack foods are made at a factory. Before they are made, people **inspect** them. Is the potato rotten? Out it goes. Is a chip a funny shape? Out! Snacks in clumps go out, too. Only perfect chips and snacks go into a bag.

The inspectors have good eyesight!

Food Stylist

A food stylist **prepares** food for photos. Sounds easy. It's not. The food is under hot lights. It starts to look bad fast. Corn flakes get soggy. What will the stylist do? Use white glue instead of milk!

Good to Know

Food stylists have a tool kit. They may need toothpicks, paint, cardboard, and more!

A stylist uses her tools on a burger. Cold cheese goes on the burger. A hot knife melts the edges. Pickle, tomato, and lettuce go on next. Pins hold them in place. Where's the ketchup? In an eyedropper. *Squirt!* Great photo!

Odor Tester

An odor is a smell. So odor testers use their noses. They smell things like paint, soap, even candy. *Sniff, sniff.* Does it smell nice? If not, the tester fixes it.

Yuck becomes *Ahhh*.

Words to Know

common: ordinary, not special

dental: having to do with teeth

exercise: activity to keep fit and healthy

inspect: check something very carefully

messages: information shared in writing

prepare: to get ready

Learn More at the Library

Check out these books to learn more.

Gerry, Lisa M. *100 Things to Be When You Grow Up.* National Geographic Kids, 2017.

Shaw, Gina. *Curious About Zoo Vets* (Smithsonian). Grosset & Dunlap, 2015.

Index

About the Author

Alice Boynton has an odd job. She writes books like this one. She is an adult and likes to read big books. But when she is on the job in New York, she writes for children like you!